Month _____ Year _____

Sun	Mon	Tues	Wed	Thurs	Fri	Sat

IMPORTANT THINGS TO DO THIS MONTH

Birthdays

Medical Appointments

Date/Party Nights

Exercises

IMPORTANT THINGS TO DO
THIS MONTH

Birthdays

Medical Appointments

Date/Party Nights

Exercises

Month _____ Year _____

Sun	Mon	Tues	Wed	Thurs	Fri	Sat

www.ingramcontent.com/pod-product-compliance
Lightning Source LLC
Chambersburg PA
CBHW070438180526
45158CB00019B/1667